11 DAYS COUNT DOWN
YOUR PRESENT AND FUTURE

A MUST READ DIGEST FOR ALL! (Push To the finish Line)

11 DAYS COUNT DOWN
YOUR PRESENT AND FUTURE

11 DAYS
COUNT DOWN

YOUR FUTURE

&

PRESENT

A MUST READ DIGEST FOR ALL! (Push To the finish Line)

11 DAYS COUNT DOWN
YOUR PRESENT AND FUTURE

CONTENT

INTRODUCTION
KICK THE NORM (Garbage and Lies)
GET UP
SNAP OUT OF IT
IMAGINE
FOCUS
POINT OF CONTACT
TARGET
START NOW
DREAM
IMMEDIATE RESOURCES
PLANT
EXPECTANCY
DETERMINATION
FOLLOW THROUGH
NO MORE RESOLUTIONS
CONCLUSION

A MUST READ DIGEST FOR ALL! (Push To the finish Line)

11 DAYS COUNT DOWN
YOUR PRESENT AND FUTURE

INTRODUCTION

2013 is on the brink of coming to an end. Many individuals have being so hopeful when the year got started. Today for many, life as throne them a curve ball, that they were not able to catch or manipulate in the court. The ball was so heavy for many that, they could not shoot. So many times in life, it was not because you never got the training, or had no clue what to do. So often, things just happen, when you were working so hard to a better outcome. They are those situations especially, which may involve other people. It could have being a bank loan, for the business, a new business merger, or some other partnership, which depended on the other persons, coming through, to allow things to work out.

Most time when you have a project that required others, to see to its success, you are almost in the hands of hope and faith. The reason is, only you can truly go the extra mile no matter what it takes to make things happen. It is true, that they are individuals who believe in what you are doing, and will go the extra mile, or is deemed to be reliable, and will come through for you. While this is true, only you will get up at 2: AM, or stay up all night studying or writing the final grade paper. Only you can indeed give a better report of you, or defend yourself no matter what the cost.(Learn to own your power.)

That is the point; I am trying to get through to you. It is all about the cost. For many, there is a price tag attached to anything they are willing to do for you, or have agreed to. Only you will truly sacrifice so often, to make your dreams and aspiration come through, or that which is vitally important to you. Everyone wants to succeed at something, even if they pretend not to be. That inner interest for themselves, will cause them, to be leased interested, in whatever you've got going own. It is obvious by this that you are beginning to see the picture. You have got to take your future, and what matters to you in your own hands, and run with that baton, which is to be handed down to your children, and don't put it down, until you have successfully ran that leg of the race. (Discover Your Power within)

11 months and 19-20 days have passed by in 2013, and so many reflections of Failures, and successes lingers your mind. You may have even tried to channel the blame elsewhere, or pretend as thou, it's just another year. You may have even accepted life the way it is, believing there is no way out, especially if you have not had many celebrations or successes, this year. The question is, "What Now? or What's Next?". The answer still relies, or is rested on your shoulders. It always falls back to you. When children are involved, it means that you must find a way, to reach for your star, while coaching your children how to seek theirs, and give them incites, of how to prevent the pitfalls, you've had.

The choice is simple. You can continue accepting that 2013 must ends the way it as being, and so will 2014 trend in the same path with no achievements, or you can continue reading "11 DAYS COUNT DOWN" with a mind determine to find the path, which could get you set up, and ready to master 2014, and beyond the next 15 -20 years of your life. You owe it to yourself to take a chance, and make your dreams come through. The past is gone, and there's no way, to turn back the clock, be it that, you had, successes or not. It has the tendency to drag you down, or tries to pull along, especially if it held, bad visions, thoughts and memories. Let it go, and keep your head straight with no regrets, reaching for the top, until victory is yours. Thanks for reading, and sharing this book to the entire universe. Thank you.

A MUST READ DIGEST FOR ALL! (Push To the finish Line)

11 DAYS COUNT DOWN
YOUR PRESENT AND FUTURE

KICK THE NORM (Garbage and Lies)

Are you tired of being tired?. I know that feelings. It seems as thou, that is a part of life challenges that everyone must cope with. It is not the same dimension for everyone, but there are coping levels, that everyone is able to undergo. It is like a car, that as several different levels of driving, pertaining to the speedometer. According to the maker of the car, it's model and features, will perform differently from another. It will also be able to take on more stress, or have a longer mobile cycle, before it really requires maintenance. Especially the tough rugged trucks or caterpillars/ bulldozers, build to break building down. You could not compare such trucks to a Ferrari, in getting the job done of the bulldozer.

The same applies, that you could not expect a bulldozer, to look as beautiful as the Ferrari, with the luxurious features and speed it's normally package with. I am saying to you my friends that you are stronger than you believe you are. You have got to find your own strength, and where your talents and energy works best for you. You must stop comparing yourself with others, and not try to do what they have being doing, and expects that you will have the same outcome. Be original and find your voice. Be the pace setter, a person who make things happen positively, for growth and success..

Sometimes, it may be the exact same product, but you will not merge ahead if your skills and talent cannot reproduce it, get it marketed, and make it better. Take a look at Google, and Microsoft. Microsoft gave us the windows platform, making computing much easier. Google started up a company, and made a web Browser next to none, that even though Microsoft came out with Bing later, they are having a hard time catching up. This is because, the world trust Google Search, to provide the best information. To make it more frustrating to Bing developers, Google architects, kept finding ways to make it better every day. So Google is always trying to improve themselves, and so must you.

This leads me to the next point. Stop accepting things the way they are. It does not have to be this way. If you work for a company, and you hate the job, starting finding a way to get out. Find a way to secure another job, that is more like you, and perhaps closer to your career goals. After securing that job, then you can quit the other. The same goes for business, or if you wanted to have your own business, you must do something about it. Life is what you make it. Stop accepting the lies. Again stop accepting the lies. Get away from people who just kept feeding you with lies that life does not get better than what it is currently. No one would have started a company or purchase a house if this was factual.

So often, it's because they do not want you to succeed, above them, and so they give you the negative stories, of why you should not. Listen to your friends or those that may know your plans. The first few sentences they echoes, so often will be a discouraging tactics. They are either afraid, it could work, or you may just succeed in life. If you are part of their team, should you succeed means you will leave them, especially if you are a great asset to their group or company. "KICK THE NORM ASIDE". You are not as poor as you think. You are not as dull as you think. You are not as illiterate as you think. You may have a goal mine embedded in you, crying for expression. To realize it and bring it to life, will be another mile stone for you. When you see yourself as the president, or an executive riding a fine car, it's not just wild wishes and dreams, but it's actually within you. With help, you can get it out.

A MUST READ DIGEST FOR ALL! (Push To the finish Line)

11 DAYS COUNT DOWN
YOUR PRESENT AND FUTURE

Stop looking at your circumstances, and the many trials, errors, and failures you've had. Stop saying, this is the way life will be until you die. Stop accepting the lies, that because your mother was a hustler and your father, a drunkard, you will be the same. Stop accepting the lies that all your family has being poor for 10 generations, and so nothing will change now, except to manage until you die.
ARE YOU SERIOUS?. You do not have cancer. Only a cancer patient should or perhaps would sound like that. Even a person with very complicated cancer, will hear the advice of many; from clergy men/women, hospital support and families, encouraging the person, to be strong and be happy, even if they only have 1 minute or a second of survival left to go.

To even fight this deadly ailment, you must be strong, and not accept the fact that, there is no way out, and that all you need to do, is write the will, and prepare to die. It is all about the fight, and overcoming. You are strong men and women, with the entire future given to you for the taking, waiting for you to change your way of thinking and approach. You cannot go through life believing and accepting these lies. Stop this "NEGATIVE NORM" now, before it continues another 5 generation. I am almost at the point of tears, because you have so much greatness in you, and the world as being waiting for you.

Do not add to the statics of the grave yard, where so much potential and riches resides. "CHANGE THE NORM" . Reach for the exceptional, and begin to make the difference in your life. Keep your mind fresh, by reading positive things, and listening to people who as a similar mind set, and wants to succeed in life. If you hang around those who want to smoke all day long, and do dope, or talk about nonsense, or go girl/boy hopping, you will turn out just like them, and nothing to show. Do not desire their friendship. If life starts and stop with their sleep or drinking, seek out new friendship of those, who will strengthens, encourage and empowers you, to take a leap of faith to accomplishments.

You can push "NORM ASIDE". With just a few days left in 2013 and to anticipate the upcoming 2014, you can begin implementing the secrets of this book. Start applying yourself. Take the 11 days challenge, to make some changes in your life, for the better good and you can accomplish it. Do you really believe you cannot change "NORM" IN 11-10 DAYS"?. Think again!. Have you not read, according to the book of Genesis, that the earth was created in 6 days?. You may say it's a hoax, phony or not true!. Why did you not remain the same, when you were born? . Seriously!. On day one, you were one day old. By day 10 or 11, you were much older according to the days. "GROWTH" took place, and you started adapting to your environment, and bonding with your parents, especially your mother, though you had no clue she was.

The point is, during those days of growth, you had your vitals check, hearing, smelling, speech capabilities, eye sight check, boys had their circumcision, and so many other factors. If that was possible within the first 2-3 days of birth, why can you not change the "NORM" around you within the next 10-11 days, and begin to have a better and brighter outlook on life, pushing and thriving to accomplish more. Because no one went to College in your family, does not mean you must do the same. Getting a student loan is not a bad thing. You are smarter and greater, the more you know.

A MUST READ DIGEST FOR ALL! (Push To the finish Line)

11 DAYS COUNT DOWN
YOUR PRESENT AND FUTURE

GET UP

Trainers in physical fitness, will tell you, the process to get up is easier than sitting down . The reason is: The hamstrings, along with the erector spine (Spinal erectors) are more involved in the getting up movement, while the calves (soleus and gastrocnemius), as well as the peroneus longhorns, act to help stabilize the lower leg. Hip flexors play a more active role in the standing up movement. These muscles contract to move your hips underneath your body, (Internet, ND). This may sound like a little anatomy,(Study of the Human body). However, what I am trying to communicate to you is that, you were natural created with a built in support system, to do more than little. It is time to "GET UP". Let your thoughts, highlight the dreams you have of succeeding, as you visualize completion.

If you have never being obedient in your life, or listen to instructions, let it start now. No man is an Island, and no man stands alone. The muscles and joints, automatically respond, when you stand and sit. Allow yourself to automatically respond to the sound of success, which does require "Standing Up". This action does not always mean physically, but in your mind, your intentions, and level of understanding. "GET UP" off the coach, "GET UP" out of the bed, stop doing nothing, and begin to do something. There is a scripture, even if you are not religious, that says; "How long wilt thou sleep, O sluggard? Wilt thou arise out of thy sleep? (Proverbs 6:9). Even if you truly hate this analogy, because it is bible base, let's examine the facts. When you are sleeping, you are in one place for the most part. You are absolutely not being productive. I understand about getting rest, allowing the cells to get rejuvenated, and continue your growth process, nature wise. However, you are like logged at this point, strolling along. Things that strolled have no point of direction. Try a sleep walker, they knows best.

So often, sleeping is connected to unproductiveness or not getting things done. That is the reason why they have created so many products with caffeine, to keep the human minds alert, and so many other energy drinks, to sustain the body to get through a work week or day. Sometimes if you sleep for too long, you feel like someone has given you a slap over the head, or you are going through an hang over, for those who have experienced it before. So sleeping can be good and it can be bad. You have being sleeping excessively, and it's time to "WAKE UP", and smell the "ROSES". Rise from your slumber. You have being doing too many slumber parties, while some of your friends or acquaintances including the rest of the world is business getting successful. If you are not careful, by time you "WAKE UP" and realize it, you are the only one left behind.

1-10 days, perhaps 6 or 7 is all you have left, to change some things in your life. Can you do it? "You better know you can". It requires or takes, a self-motivated mind, and a heart sold out to progress, and a "NO LOOKING BACK" determine attitude to succeed. I wrote "NO LOOKING BACK" the way I did, to emphasize on the fact that'; if you allow yourself to remain at the place where you are, and keep accepting all that sitting down as brought you, you could become obese in your emotions, wanting to make a move, but you feel stuck, and you kept packing on the weight out of self-pity. Sometimes you may think about the reasons why you cannot, before focusing on why you should. If you have not herd, or understood anything that I have said so far, "stop for a moment, look around you, can you see yourself at the same place this time next year?. How does it look and feel?. Happy or sad, is on you.

A MUST READ DIGEST FOR ALL! (Push To the finish Line)

11 DAYS COUNT DOWN
YOUR PRESENT AND FUTURE

SNAP OUT OF IT

Here are some statics for you concerning day dreaming, or a sense of movement, like a toy with no gain. **Unlike previous thought, the universal phenomenon of daydreaming is a normal part of our cognitive processes. Daydreaming is defined as "spontaneous, subjective experiences in a no-task, no stimulus, no-response situation…[and] includes unintended thoughts that intrude inadvertently into the execution of intended mental tasks… and undirected ideas in thought sampling during wakefulness". Although a single daydream usually lasts only a few minutes, it is estimated that we spend one-third to one-half of our waking hours daydreaming, although that amount can vary significantly from person to person, (DUJS, 2011).**

In contrast to what its name may suggest, daydreaming seems to be quite different from the dreams experienced during sleep. Another interesting fact about daydreaming is that "the seemingly continual stream of consciousness is discontinuous, consisting of a sequence of concatenated, psychophysiological building blocks … that follow each other in fractions of seconds". Daydreaming is often looked down upon, as John McGrail, a Los Angeles clinical hypnotherapist, explains: "Daydreaming is looked upon negatively because it represents 'non-doing' in a society that emphasizes productivity…. We are under constant pressure to do, achieve, produce, and succeed" . Sigmund Freud even believed that fantasies were the creations of the unfulfilled, and that daydreaming and fantasy were early signs of mental illness, (DUJS, 2011).

I am not about to discuss the findings of the experts, or argue with them concerning this matter. However take a look at one of the statements. It said Mr. Sigmund Freud, as being an expert in the field, argued that, day dreaming was the early sign for mental issues. Perhaps because it looks like it, that only comes naturally I suppose. The fact is, stop looking like someone in a Trans, being hypnotize by another person or thing, twirled up in day dreaming. When that happens, nothing gets done, and people could literally break in your house, and steal whatever they wanted.

Are you going to allow 2013 to end, and you are still daydreaming or in a Trans. I do not care if it happens naturally according to some people. The fact is, if it's not putting you on the path of production and to get active towards success, then it's doing you no good. So I say; "SNAP OUT OF IT". You seem to be awake! Thou sleep lingers. Are you a Zombie?, I know you're not. For the records, Zombies are for cartoons fairy tale. It is not real at all. You are a real person, and never should you be compared to this fictitious character. Loose the nonchalant behavior, and get a sense of purpose and direction in your life "SNAP OUT OF IT". It is time to have finish your inventory, and the stock taking, to analyzed where you are in life, to throw out the trash, and to pick up yourself, and begin to run . Get your sonic speed on, and get moving.

To change your life, and circumstances around you, is a choice. You can stay in your Trans, or day dream, being hypnotized by the reality of life. This could be because you're not able to pay your bills, shop for your kids, go to school, make your car payment, and the list goes on. However, you can choose to "SNAP OUT OF IT" do something radical before the year gets done, that even if you do not start making money right away, you will at-lease be positioned for a better 2014.

A MUST READ DIGEST FOR ALL! (Push To the finish Line)

11 DAYS COUNT DOWN
YOUR PRESENT AND FUTURE

IMAGINE

Imagination comes with a certain sense of hope. It's to be in the process of imagining something. To form a mental picture of, to think or believe, (Kares, 2008). Amazing enough, how the world was created from the concept of imagination. Yeah ! Some of you will say it's science, some will say evolution. The fact is, before mankind, or human existence on Planet earth, so many things were not in place. Can you imagine living in a world, where you had was to rub sticks together on a stone, or something so as to get light?. Can you imagine having to dry wood by some means, and get a fire going before you could even get warm?. Can you imagine going out to the fields and killing a sheep, and cut away the skin, so you could use it for a coat, in order not to freeze to death?.

I just got you to exercise what it means to imagine. The fact is, you must learn how to actually picture a thing, before you can obtain it. It is almost a natural process. Sometimes you do not even realize that you were doing it. However, they are different levels. You could say, it could be intentional or non-intentional. There is the process call thinking, which is necessary to get to the point of forming an image to your goals, business or aspiration. I want to focus a bit on Cognitive thinking. Everything you are about to see from the experts, I feel it is necessary, to help you cross over, into better thinking.

Which cognitive skills are most important for success?

Since the brain is such a sophisticated organ, learning is a complex process. Many interrelated cognitive skills contribute to academic and occupational success. Broadly categorized, these critical skills include: Attention, Working Memory, Processing Speed, Long-Term Memory, Visual Processing, Auditory Processing, Logic and Reasoning. These skills are interdependent. Often they overlap in their work with other skills, as all the bits of information entering the mind are processed and acted upon. **Define Cognitive Thinking — The Connection to Learning.** The detailed list that follows shows how each skill connects to the learning task it enables. The strength or weakness of one skill impacts the general effectiveness of other skills.

Attention: Sustained Attention enables you to stay on task for a period of time.

- Selective Attention enables you to stay on task even when a distraction is present.

- Divided Attention allows you to handle two or more tasks at one time.

What to watch for: The inability to stay on task for long periods of time, to ignore distractions, or to multi-task will limit the student's other cognitive skills—which will impact all academic areas.

Working memory: Working Memory is the ability to retain information for short periods of time while processing or using it.

What to watch for: Learning suffers if information cannot be retained long enough to handle it properly.

Processing speed: Processing Speed is the rate at which the brain handles information.

A MUST READ DIGEST FOR ALL! (Push To the finish Line)

11 DAYS COUNT DOWN
YOUR PRESENT AND FUTURE

What to watch for: If processing speed is slow, the information held in working memory may be lost before it can be used, and the student will have to begin again.

Long-Term memory: Long-Term Memory is the ability to both store and recall information for later use.

What to watch for: If the ability to store and retrieve information is poor, wrong conclusions and wrong answers will result.

Visual Processing: Visual Processing is the ability to perceive, analyze, and think in visual images. Visual Discrimination is seeing differences in size, color, shape, distance, and the orientation of objects. Visualization is creating mental images.

What to watch for: When visual imagery is poor, tasks like math word problems and comprehension, which require seeing the concept/ object in the student's mind, are difficult.

Auditory Processing: Auditory Processing is the ability to perceive, analyze, and conceptualize what is heard and is one of the major underlying skills needed to learn to read and spell.

•Auditory Discrimination is hearing differences in sounds, including volume, pitch, duration, and phoneme. Phonemic Awareness is the ability to blend sounds to make words, to segment sounds, to break words apart into separate sounds, and to manipulate and analyze sounds to determine the number, sequence, and sounds within a word.

What to watch for: If blending, segmenting, and sound analysis are weak, sounding out words when reading and spelling will be difficult and error-prone.

Logic and reasoning: Logic and Reasoning skills are the abilities to reason, prioritize, and plan.

What to watch for: If these skills are not strong, academic activities such as problem solving, math, and comprehension will be difficult, (Gibson,2013).

I just gave up, more than half of my page, or writing time, to Dr. Ken, a guy I do not know, for your sake. It's because I want you to understand how to apply these methods, and change your level or method of imagination, to pull in good result. You got to think fast, and let things process quickly. Focus a lot on the Visual process. It will encourage, and possible prompts you, to exercise this method to become more visual, and connect the dots together, even before the actual project as being completed. Perhaps you need to go back to school, or you are now in school, but they are some challenges, regarding the way you learn. Keep looking back over these cognitive processes, and thrive.

Do you really believe, that if you start to put this book in practice or the, methods you see here, it will not work for you?. The doubters will say; "no, before they even take a look at it. They say it will never work, before they gave it a chance. My friends this is all about you. Give yourself the chance to explore and to get something constructively done before the year gets out. Can you do it? I know you can. Give yourself a break. It could be a wage increase, a new job, or a total new you. Start your imagination.

A MUST READ DIGEST FOR ALL! (Push To the finish Line)

11 DAYS COUNT DOWN
YOUR PRESENT AND FUTURE

FOCUS

There is another word, that reminds me easily of focus, and it's called; "concentrate". You may hear another person say; "Zoom In". Let's examine for a little, what it means to focus. According to the oxford dictionary, "focal Point" is also another way of saying focus. The definition given by the Oxford Dictionary says; "It is the center of interest or activity. Two examples given by the definition is that, (1) this generation has made the environment a focus of attention. The second is, an act of concentrating interest or activity on something,(Oxford, 2013).

By this, you do get the point of what I am trying to say. I know I am not your school teacher, your mother or your father. A total stranger I am, who wants you to succeed in life. What have you focused on, the entire 2013?. So often you either cannot answer the question, or your thoughts have just being all around the world, and therefore had not focus on one set thing. It is OK. I say again, it is OK!. There is no point trying to cry over spill milk, or beat on yourself, for something that you cannot regain the time or moment of. By the way; let me just say this; "time waits on no man, and so you must make use of every moment that you have. Your time is precious. What does your time means to you?.

For some people, especially those in the business world, time means money. Money does better when it equals assets, and trust funds. The honest truth is, we all waste valuable time doing things that is of no progress to our lives on a daily basis. The world is rotating. It is spinning on an axis, and going very fast.. Life cycles matters with this world view process. If you misuse time, it is like having the sub-way train leaving you, because you were late. Waiting for the other train, could mean, you may loose your job, spend more money, loose a promotion and so many other factors, because you were late.

That's how it is when you do not focus, and by time some thing or someone gets your attention , it could be too late. Let's take your job for example, perhaps you've being going late, perhaps you have not being performing. Management spoke to you about it, but you did not get your focus together, because of distraction. The end result will speak for itself. You're likely to be fired, loose your bonus, get suspended, or get transferred to an area you despised. The picture is clear, to visualize your surrounding and pay attention, is critical to your success, in anything and in any industry. I want you to "FOCUS RIGHT NOW". The sun knows when to rise, and you need to act on your behalf.

Take a look at the business you have always wanted to do. Call up the college or university you have always wanted to attend. Knock on the door of that job, you have always wanted even thou, they told you no before. Examine and think about, all you wanted was to do, when the year got started, and go do them now. Get rid of logic's. Logic's will tell you, if you could not get it done in 11 months, a few weeks and some days to go, before the year ends, how is it possible now. You will be amazed, what you can do, so long as you put your heart, & mind in it. You've got nothing to loose. Nothing at all to loose!. The worst thing that can happen is that, you did not get as far as you wanted to, but you got something done, that you did not do all year long. Procrastination is a beast. You must disassociate yourself from that beast, and learn how to attend to issue of your life immediately. Get busy.

A MUST READ DIGEST FOR ALL! (Push To the finish Line)

11 DAYS COUNT DOWN
YOUR PRESENT AND FUTURE

POINT OF CONTACT

Now would be a good time, for you to pull out your list. I am making mention of your contact list, from Facebook, Yahoo, G-Mail, Google Plus, AOL, Bing/Microsoft and every other personal contact you have made. The question is; who do you know, that is at the chain of command for a company, that can possible connect you?. Have you even thought of asking them for a favor?. Who is in the industry where, you have always wanted to get a career in, and you have never known how to access that point of contact, and ask how to get in. Now is the time to find their email, find their contact number, and begin to push until something great happens. Sometimes you never know, what will happen until you try.

There was a guy, that had a very thriving business or organization, he was going bankrupt, or was about to do so. He used up his life line, (VIP Contact List), and allowed his colleague; to know what was going on. The friend stood before those who could help, and ask the general population to reach out and save is company. The money he needed was raised at the last minute, and still today the organization is thriving. I would advise you, do not just keep phone numbers and emails, without separating, the important ones, from that which is just casual. I am simple saying, create a method, to identify which of your contacts are business affiliated, social, family, those who are financially stable, by their companies, and have a compassionate heart to help.

This is a very practical approach, and there is a point in your life, when you must learn how to be practical. I hope I have gotten your attention, and you are ready to go through your list. You may say, every one as done their shopping for the Christmas, and they are getting ready for the new year, so what can I do, to get their attention to help. It does not have to be monetary. It can simple be that they are willing to connect you, to the right source, who can help you out. It is all about who you know. It is not so much who knows you. Sometimes they are people who know you, but where you want to go, they cannot go with you, because they are simply going to hold you back. The best thing to do, in this aspect, is to upgrade your connection list, all the way to the white house.

Now you are saying, how is that possible?. Isn't there any one that you know in the army, that might be station at the white house?. Perhaps they know somebody who does. You could set up a tour, because it's public property, if you have the right pass, then you could get to walk around the white house. If you go on the hill, where congress is, and you know how to hold a conversation about political issues, or it could just be a question to your congress man or senator, it is only natural; you will get a new contact directly to the congress, or senate, if you care to. Any contacts you want is yours. The truth is, they are some connections or contacts, that the moment you see the name of the person, their phone number, and or email, it has $$$$ signs all over it.

I urge you, to stop and think; "which is the one number you could call, that potentially can change your life"?. It could also be one email, or a text message. It could also be one official letter professionally drafted with your resume attached, that could open the door for you, and new opportunities for 2014. If you have no one, or contacts. Use data base at the court house, and start talking to people to find leads.

A MUST READ DIGEST FOR ALL! (Push To the finish Line)

11 DAYS COUNT DOWN
YOUR PRESENT AND FUTURE

TARGET

It is very important, to talk about targeting. They are so many people that wanted to go into business for themselves or get a new job including a career, but did not know how to go about it. One of the biggest mistakes or pitfalls, is when the individuals, were trying to get started, and they were all over the place, without any targeted market or a niche community. The fact is, even thou you like Foreign currency trading, or other stock exchange, possible E-bay, or Amazon, It is very important to stick to one area, where you can learn all about it, and begin your marketing strategies.

When you have identified a niche market especially if you wanted to start a business, it will be easier to target those people, on the Internet, instead of trying to reach the entire population. Why a niche group?. If you are selling (Ads) per click for example, the more your (Ads) shows up in the right place, to those who needs to see it, and your potential customers clicks on it, and then shares it with someone else, and possible it goes viral, then it generates more sales for you. If you were trying to sell cruise, or vacation packages, targeting the "baby boomers" or the "newly graduates" especially during spring break, the "TARGETED APPROACH" would be more effective.

For those that have being trying to get a career change, or find a way to increase their earning potentials, it is very important to find one career path, and stick to it. It is true that, you may be a qualified manager, or perhaps you are so knowledgeable that you could swing or juggle more than one career path at the same time. However, there is a saying that comes from the older folks. "You have become jack of all trades, and master of none". This simple means, all these things you can do, but you have not mastered any of them. You are like a swing in the wind that tosses back and forth, according to the motion or direction of the wind. Does this kind of unproductive behavior or pattern sounds like you?. If it does, then it's time to change it. Such behavior could have being your 2013 downfall.

If you are a victim of not targeting a career, or niche group for your business, and stick to it, it's not too late. It is never too late. Right now, can you take out your pencil, or pen, and a clean sheet of paper, and do an exercise with me. Create two columns at the top of the sheet, and write (First Career choice). Next you will write (Other career choices). Go ahead and list one career that you are passionate about, and you will give it your all. Now write out the other possibilities under other career choices. You are writing those down, not to focus on them, but for later reference, when you have mastered your first career, perhaps time allows you, to do another job on the side, then you could go back to that list.

Do the same for a company you would like to start. (Write the kind of business and then list a few others to add to your successful business, which might be compatible, or perhaps a different business). I guarantee you, if you take these steps to accomplish the task accordingly, you will see result in early 2014. It is also possible to get a website up and running in these few days to go. It is also possible to identify your "Target market or Niche". It is also possible to seek out the best approach to your career path, and the quickest way to get it done, without becoming frustrated or discourage. All this is possible, if you make use of this information and begin "Targeting". You owe it to yourself.

A MUST READ DIGEST FOR ALL! (Push To the finish Line)

11 DAYS COUNT DOWN
YOUR PRESENT AND FUTURE

START NOW

This is a call to action. To get to the end of anything, there must be a beginning. Let us use the approach of your daily commute. Perhaps it's going to work, church, school, or where ever your travels may take you. There is a routine of getting up, perhaps, you had breakfast, and concluded on your attire. It is also required, that before you can go anywhere, you will need to start the car, or walk to the train station or bus stop. Sometimes it requires you, to call a cab. Whatever method you use on a daily basis, it does not happens automatically. You must first do something, and then the others will follow. Sometimes starting seems so difficult. Have you experienced that? I know you have.

There is a way of getting over that stigma, or doubt, and is by looking at those who are currently doing the same thing, you have wanted to get done, and who are possible role models to you. When you admire someone a lot and look up to them, it is easy to be inspired, by what they are doing. Today, I am asking you, to find someone, of influence, and become inspired today. Motivation is needed, to start anything. For many, the method of how they become motivated is different. Some people is motivated, by the skills they will learn from the career opportunity. For others, it could be money or financial gain, and then for others, it could be extending their resume, by the caliber of people they will meet. Resume, does not only constitute, work and school history/career. Try those of great connections, it's amazing.

It does not matter what gets you going, or excites you, it is time to get connected to it. There are many that have lost their passion, or is just being demotivated all through the year. There is no time, to continue being sad about one thing or the other. If you are feeling low at heart or in spirit/vibes, figure out what is causing it, and amend it immediately. Negative feelings will prevent you, from starting anything at this moment, towards the elevation of your life. This kind of weakness doesn't care attitude, will lead you nowhere at all. Especially during this season, with so many holidays, it is natural that all you may want to do is hang out with friends, family, relax and just have a good time.

This season is going to pass, and when it does, will you kick the curve wall, and said';" I wish I had taken Paul Powell advise, in 11 Days Count Down" and make a change. Do not find yourself living moments of regrets, it is time to celebrate you and success. Learn how to start good and end well. You can get away from the noise and distractions for a bit, and start figuring out, how to take advantage of this book. I did the same thing. I tuned out everything, and got to my writing studio, and began putting this book together, so you can have it, to make an investment in yourself. If I did it, so can you.

The excitement is momentary, but in just a few days, you will have no choice but to welcome 2014. What will your future look like then?, what will your present look like then?. If you make a go at it now, you are going to start feeling so good about yourself that you started a process, with your name on it, and it leads to a better place of stability, financial growth, and independence. I cannot say this enough that, you must tune out anything and any one, who will tell you, it is not possible. Anything is possible if only you believe, and put your heart in it. It is time to give yourself a financial make over, but it requires a person oriented for success. Do one thing; "START NOW"

A MUST READ DIGEST FOR ALL! (Push To the finish Line)

11 DAYS COUNT DOWN
YOUR PRESENT AND FUTURE

DREAM

To allow your dreams to actualize, and release economic power, you must clearly understand your past, present and future. It is a nonstarter, to dwell on your past. It does not matter how bad it was, get over it and move on. It deviates from the dreams of succeeding, and your goal objectives. With a consciousness of deliberately hanging on to the past, creates a distraction for yourself to discover the inner you, and give voice to your deepest desires, that only you could bring to light for the world to see.

When you spend time reflecting on your pass experiences, which lead to your dreams not coming through, you are doing and serving yourself injustice, believing it can't and won't happen now. Sometimes, you are your biggest obstruction to your success. Are you not tired of playing the blame game? Look around you, and you will notice, the clock is ticking. You are not getting younger, no matter what your age is, and you must begin to take responsibility for where you are now in life, and make a U-Turn.

Yes, I know it's hard, and you cannot believe it, because you are so qualified, and you ended up at a car wash place, where you make an income. You are so talented, and so smart, yet you are working among the UN-intelligent, school drop outs, no GED individuals in a warehouse, or on the assembly line. Let it humbles you, clear your head, and use it for a stepping stone, to get back to your original plans of becoming the next Oprah Winfrey, Barack Obama, Nelson Mandela, or who so ever, and whatever you inspired to be. The worst thing you could do at this point, is say; "it does not matter anymore". Remember this, you are not the owner of the company, where you are making just enough to help pay the bills. Also, any job that they can teach, or show someone how to do the task, is not a career. It means they can fire you at any given moment, and replaces you dime and a dozen (many choices).

Here's what I want you to do; create a system, to pick up on yourself, or catch yourself, whenever you are about to travel in the pass negative dark ages of your life. "STOP" flick on the light switch in the present immediately. It does not matter if you've being divorce, you are a single mother or father including the fact that, you kept losing your job. Sometimes going back in your mind, and the ugly fear of experiencing the same, actually allow you to mess up again, or just simply stop performing, and waiting to get fired. That's not living. You have strength in abundance, which dominates the fear.

Whatever you continuously focus on, will be the reflection or outcome of your life. You cannot put a bad injection in your system, and expects the outcome will be great. It is like focusing on crack or cocaine, which equals addiction, and the loss of everything from that point. You may even die while trying to get high, drugging it out. Repeating the pass is a result of continuously highlighting such happenings or doings. Stop allowing history to repeats itself. Own your power.

"But how can I learn from my mistakes if I don't look back?" Although this question seems to be the excuse line for most of you, don't add to statistics. Do not allow lack or fear, to imposed constant habit of looking back, because in your mind, It is the only way of acknowledging your mistakes, and learn how not to repeat them. This pattern of thinking puts your mind process on the Ferris wheel. Your mind

A MUST READ DIGEST FOR ALL! (Push To the finish Line)

11 DAYS COUNT DOWN
YOUR PRESENT AND FUTURE

just kept twirling around or spinning, then it creates a negative cycle, and by time you get off, 30 years of your life as passed, with no improvements. The moment failure or mistake unravels, absorbed it for that moment, then suppress it, after talking about it, or whatever works to releases it from your inner system. Clear your pallet. The pallet of your mind and emotions, and prepare to welcome the new. Failure as many calls it, is just an opportunity for an adjustment. If you do not find the channel to fix or adjust the failures, it could lead to poverty, which as many negative side effects. You are a person who is not perfect, and indeed we live in an UN-perfect world. To feel bad, when your efforts, were not awarded, may just be a natural process. Looking in the mirror, reflects a person, of hope and strength.

It's natural sometimes, wanting comfort like a baby. However, you must let that moment pass very quickly. Become independent, and an analyst of your actions. Evaluate why it did not work out. Do your research, and learn what adjustments, can be made to the product, relationship, company, life style, and dressing, to have a better outcome next time. Thomas Edison is known for the one who created the light-bulb. The fact is, it was a laboratory experiment. Many others were working at that project, trying to find the right material that would allow the electrical light bulb to work. In 1878, Mr. Edison, believes that he could solve the problem, and create a better light bulb.

He tried and tried, some would have said; he failed. However his techniques and plans, just needed an adjustment, including hiring a Princeton graduate. Some times in life, to get ahead, or to succeed you must seek out a professional in that sector, who can help you to achieve your goals. Not everything in life is free. Most time to get the best quality, you must find the financial investment from somewhere to invest in your future. In 1879 Thomas Edison staff saw results of things changing. Changes may not happen overnight, and for the most part they never do. We are living in a microwave, quick fix microorganism society, and it leads to nothing long term, but just temporary. You can allow your dreams to become a reality, chartering the right path, which will leave a trail behind for generations to come.

Although Thomas Edison had invented the Stock Picker, Phonograph, telegraph and the mimeograph, only the incandescent light-bulb, are still in use today. I hope you have picked up on something here. Thompson Edison got the fame, and world artifacts recognition, for being the creator of light-bulbs, when he actually just found the secret, after trying 1000 times for the incandescent bulbs. My fellow readers, it does not matter where you live in the world, look around you, look in the work place, the television, and for those in school, the laboratory. You can take anything, improve on it, and become financially wadded from it, and get some accolades and honor, while doing it.

For your information; Face-Book, was not Mark zuckerberg idea in the first place. He went to Harvard, and the fraternity, or some social group, knew he had some knowledge in the ++ script programming technique. They ask him to use his skills and make the school social website much better. He went to his room, and for many days, and weeks, there was no sign of Mark on Campus. During this time, he was in his room, with his roommate, creating Face-Book. You can imagine that he also stole the initial sign ups as well, that was in the school database. If he stole the concept and made it better, obviously he borrowed everything else. Since stole is too much of a harsh word. My friends he had a dream

A MUST READ DIGEST FOR ALL! (Push To the finish Line)

11 DAYS COUNT DOWN
YOUR PRESENT AND FUTURE

embedded in his system, that no one saw, or knew about except him. People tense to have a short memory, because thou unethical it was what he did, the entire world have forgotten about it, and never saw it as a big deal. Everywhere you go today is Face-Book, enough that today it is also traded on the world stock exchange market, because of the community users, which are millions, and money it takes in monthly and quarterly for advertisements. I am not asking you to do anything unethical. How you go about it is up to you. But you got to let the voice of your dream speak out with substance. The world will not use it, see it, or appreciate it, if it stays locks up in you, and go back to the grave yard. Sorry to sound harsh, but that's exactly where it will go at the end of the day, especially not shared with the world.

Steve Jobs got his out, leaving the world with one of the finest product ever, called the Apple brand. You got an Apple brand in you, a candy brand, Julia Band, Keneisha, or Chin Brand, perhaps a Kalecia Brand, and should I say, "Junior Technical supplies" and "Jude Technologies". I am sure you have gotten the picture by this. Take a chance, and pull your dreams out. Worry about the consequences later, if there will be one. Fear and everything else in-between, leaves dream hanging in the wind by a thread.

The very Internet, you are now using was also an army experiment. Yes it was. Research it for yourself. Eventually they decide to give access to the world, and what a phenomenal saber space. It sure as made many rich and famous and you have a stake in it too. Justin Beaver must give thanks for the Internet every day, and YouTube. The young Canadian made his debut, there, singing one of Chris Brown's song, and a Good Samaritan name Usher, discovered him, and helped to make him a success story. You are a success story. You never know what lies beyond the mountain till you reach the top.
Use the negative experience or failure, as an opportunity to learn and the negative past will lose its grips and power from over your life. Let your thoughts come in subjection to positive thinking.

There is something spectacular and amazing about the future, It is a blank slate, and with an opened mind, they are so many opportunities, creativity, exploration, development and discoveries awaiting you. Releasing yourself to the future does not dictate fear. Tell the pass goodbye, and unveil the future, each day. For many, the future is not yet here, but every day you will learn to chip away a bit of it. There is a word called faith. Naturally faith shows up especially in moments of need. It is simple when you believe something can happen, or is there when it is not. Though it is dominated by the religious arena, when you go to your car and put the key in the ignitions, you are expecting it to start. That is a little faith. You get off the bed, and without looking, you places your feet down, expecting the floor to still be there, that is faith. When you purchase a ticket for the movies, expecting the show to be there, because the theater said so, and other advertisement, that's a little faith.

Use that faith, to fuel and power the future, expecting a gigantic outcome, not known to mankind or the 21st century. Think big, think positive, think realistic. Let your dream frightens you, but excites at the same time, with much enthusiasm to get it out. Power your dream to success. Let the Past be a reflection of an illusion. These thoughts live in the mind and so, controlling them, helps to reflect or influence the outcome of your dreams this very moment. Be it quantum physics, philosophy, or psychology, they are proof, that the president will make significant alteration to the past.

A MUST READ DIGEST FOR ALL! (Push To the finish Line)

11 DAYS COUNT DOWN
YOUR PRESENT AND FUTURE

Challenge yourself, and initialize these words to power the mental state of your mind, as you visualize your dreams in the present, which will eventually command action, for the future this very moment as you focus. These are power nuggets to your success. You must utilize them.

Level 1: Launch Your Courage
Reason: It gives you the courage to dream, or to have a vision. (Not the sleeping dream or vision)
Level 2: Drive Your Desires
Reason: Activate your conscious belief systems. Be bold about it, and make no apologies.
Level 3: Free Your Imagination
Reason: Imagination stimulates, and stirs up the ability to discover the dream.
Level 4: Stage Your Dream
Reason: Enlightened visualization, as you see it coming to pass.
Level 5: Pen Your Dream Script
Reason: Power of words-write it. Make it plain, one day the voice of it, shall be herd, thou delayed.
Level 6: Set Your Dream on Fire
Reason: Ignite dream momentum, and put action to it now, not tomorrow.
Level 7: Publish Your Dream Plan Book
Reason: Connect with the "Thinking Stuff", get it in a journal, or any paper, paste on wall to see them.
Level 8: Inspire Your Dream with Action
Reason: Power of the present moment. To do nothing, is a formula for permanent failure without help.
Level 9: Awaken Your Dream with Thanks
Reason: Attraction action of gratitude. Start appreciating, the dreams, and celebrate the expectations.
Level 10: Become a Dream Achiever
Reason: Live, share, expand your dreams. the sky is the limit. The opportunities are vast, get yours.

This chapter will prove to be the longest, which is for a reason. Everything in life, starts with a dream, or a kind of supernatural enhancement, to your thoughts, that will give room, to explore the beyond. If no one had the ability to dream, visualize, imagine, coordinate, and bring it to actualization, from the picture or image, they first saw, in the mind, through the dream process, nothing would have being around today. Things such as cell phones, TV, a house, car, and the list are very easy to make. There is no other way to say this; "if you want to change your life, own a financial portfolio, leverage your investments, become stable and, go wherever, having more buying power, you must let your dreams come alive. If you have no dreams, visions, or goals, I urge you, to start dreaming my friend.

A MUST READ DIGEST FOR ALL! (Push To the finish Line)

11 DAYS COUNT DOWN
YOUR PRESENT AND FUTURE

IMMEDIATE RESOURCES

Everyone has access to the internet. If it's not on your laptops, it's on your Desk Top or Pc, Tablets, IPhones, Blackberries and your androids. You have them all, which gives quick access by way of a 4g network to any information you so desire to have. Use one of these devices, and search the web for new opportunities. The internet as a gold mine of quality information ready to make you so much cash, than you have ever had. Here are a few examples. If you want to work with children, possible start up a daycare business or any other industry, it is waiting for you.

Daycare: www.SBA.gov, www.childcare.gov , where you can learn how to start up a business of this nature. If you want to go back to school to earn a degree, it can be done today anywhere from around the world. Here are 2 sources, www.capella.edu, www.waldenn.edu, for a larger database listing of schools, go to www.onlinecolleges.net. If you like media, blogging or talk show, you can start on the internet. For a talk show, you could use, www.blogtalkradio.com. It is free to sign up, and you will get your own phone numbers, to actually have a live talk show, like any other professionals in the field. The better or more syndicated your material is, and the topics you talk about, could allow your show to pull traction and begin making money. It's really all up to you. If you want to be on TV, or start a show like any other professionals such as Oprah Winfrey it is possible. Get a video recorder, which is available on your phone as well, and record yourself, interviewing some body or talking about a topic.

Go to www.livestream.com, and create your own TV Channel. You do not have to pay for this channel either, unless you want to go professional which is not recommended, unless you have the audience and advertisement to run, which will create revenue. If you want to be on radio, as in your own radio station, go to www.shoutcast.com. You will need to register a domain, to look more professional, but it is not a must, because you can pay the low fee at shoutcast.com, and use a blogging community such as www.bloggerspot.com, to show case your radio station. You will need some other equipment, to sound professional, which can be purchase at low prices. The question raveling your mind, is how can money be made from this?. If you have professional content on all of these platforms, and you stood out among the rest, then you can attract advertisers, who will pay you up to $5000 for one Ads. It takes hard work, but it is possible.

If you want to be a writer, soft wares are available to get you going. You can use the notepad on your computer and also any other word document to write with. Most of these software, are also word editors, which can and will help you accomplish your goals. After you are through writing the best novel ever, you can submit it to www.createspace.com, and www.outskirtspress.com. you'll then keep all the royalties. If you are ready to go big time, then use www.tatepublishing.com, who can help you. Do your research and find other sources to accomplish your heart desires. For a new career, you can search with www.indeed,com, www.beyond.com, and so many others. If you need a business plan to be drafted, use www.masterplans.com, or www.growthink.com. A professional resume, can be created at; www.myperfectresume.com. I just prove to you, that the Internet is a pool of resources, that any area of business you want to pursue can be done. Make me proud and be the next success story.

A MUST READ DIGEST FOR ALL! (Push To the finish Line)

11 DAYS COUNT DOWN
YOUR PRESENT AND FUTURE

PLANT

There is a basic rule, when it implies to planting. If you do not put anything in the ground, then it means you will not be able to harvest anything. It is straight forward. I am aware of the fact, that they are times, when you reap or harvest and you were not the one, who planted anything. However, the general rule is, you will reap the same as you have sown, and enjoy the benefits or the fruits thereof. Planting and investing, work together interchangeable. They are many things which must be considered, before you invest or plant. I will differentiate them both, and illustrate.

CONDITIONS FOR PLANTING

According to the expert, here is an intro, of what's required. When establishing a new date plantation, certain actions need to be implemented to ensure the long term success of the plantation. One of these actions involves the initial land preparation which should be done prior to transplanting of the plant material (offshoots or tissue culture-derived plants). The purpose of land preparation is to provide the necessary soil conditions which will enhance the successful establishment of the young offshoots or the tissue culture plants received from the nursery. Considering the nature of the date palm, one cannot "save" on this operation and hope for long term sustainability of the plantation. The aim is to enable the date grower to plan and structure the implementation process in advance, ensuring the successful establishment of the date plantation. Planning forms part of the initial preparation and will help to limiting unnecessary stoppages during the implementation phase,(Klein & Zaid, ND).

Critical factors to consider during this planning exercise are summarized as follows:

- Availability and quality of irrigation water;
- Field selection;
- Mechanical actions to be implemented;
- Chemical needs for pre-plant soil improvement;
- Tools and equipment needed for date cultivation;
- Labor needs;
- Irrigation design and installation;
- Leaching schedule;
- Hole preparation;
- Financial requirements and
- Time schedule.

There is a reason why I took the time to outline the process of planting, by those in the field. You will realize something that, you cannot just plant into any soil, without adequate preparation to accommodate the outcome you have being expecting. The list clearly gives you the formula. Water is a must, even if the best land was not selected. The chemical, tools, labor, time and financial obligations, must be accounted for. When you take the bold step to launch something for the first time, you must consider these same things similarly to planting. You must ensure, your plan is practical and feasible (doable). You must ensure that, if it is a new business, that you have a business plan drafted, how you plan on acquiring the funding, who will be your board of directors, and help in the business, how much cash flow is currently at hand, the location for the business, your target market, or preferred customers, and to get your business fully licensed, or incorporated.

A MUST READ DIGEST FOR ALL! (Push To the finish Line)

11 DAYS COUNT DOWN
YOUR PRESENT AND FUTURE

It may sound like a lot, but it's a little fraction compare to the success you will have later, once the project gets off the ground. At first it is a project, because you are testing the waters to see how things go for you. All that you have just done, if you followed those steps, it's planting a business in or on mother earth, where you can expects to harvest from at a later date. It is the same process of reaping and harvesting. If you put nothing in mother earth, then you cannot expect to get anything back. You must also be prepared, to be patient with the business for at least two-three years, before you have possible paid off the loans, and settle the agreement with investors, and then starts to see some real profit. I would advise you that during your business startup, and for the first two years, keep your living arrangements, the same as they were. Do not increase your cost, by taking out luxury car loan against the business, or start eating out every night, and start throwing parties. Be very discipline, maintain and manage things the way they were, until the business as truly becomes yours.

I mentioned ownership, because if the loan was guaranteed by the business, it is actually not yours until you have paid off the loan. It is like a car payment, if the payments are not made, and get there on time, you run the risk of losing the car. There is no difference to the rule for the business. If you just acquired a new job, which might have being an high profile job, you need to put in the work or time required to succeed. Find out everything about the culture of the company, the job you will be performing, and how to go above and beyond your employers' expectations. With the time and quality efforts invested, you will harvest later. This could be in the form of promotion, a wage increase and naturally your paycheck as promise. If you are going to try out for a professional sports team, you also need to put time in practicing to become the best. Learn the culture of the sports team, and what they are really looking for. Learn from those who made the team previously, to find out exactly what they all have in common. If you realize you are lacking that skill or quality, no matter how good you are, do not lie to yourself, just work on getting that skill or quality, and you will stand a better chance to land the deal.

Any industry you go to, even if you are going o be an actress, or an actor, they may have taught you how to act, but without your personality getting connected to the script and owning the part, you will never get the part. The difference between you and the 1000 of other well trained candidates, who is via for the same spot will be your personality. When your personality speaks, it may just be the additional perk, the movie producers/directors were looking for. If your business is online base, then you also need to put the time and professionalism in it to make sure it works out for you. Starting a website is just not enough. You need to learn how to promote the site, the best product that is search for on the web. This will be a trending product, and how to get traffic and build back links to your site to get the sale. Customers are very impatient, and so, the moment they land on your website, it needs to be appealing. The site must be easy to navigate, organized properly, and the landing page, has all the information about the item you want to be sold, with a payment tab, ready to go. A quick check out process always beat, allowing the customer to be routed many places before completing the process.

When you invest in the stock market, it is like planting. They are some conditions which must be put in place, or will be required, to choose a good stock, and make a profit. From previous experience, you may need to set up a brokerage account. You must have access to search the database for current stocks trading, and the ones which are popular, to that of risky trading. Should I say thou, that everything is risky when it comes to trading. They are no guarantees. When you are trading, be it currency, coal, gold, or whatever; you need to know when to buy, and when to sell. This could and will be the difference between you making millions, or just a dime and a nickel. Knowing the market is crucial, and thou this can be done automatically, and you just watch the market to see how things are trending, you still need to plant or invest your time, with the expectations, you will cash out at the end of the day. Most importantly, just plant, or invest something. It is like having $10 to withdraw from the bank, compared to $0. I prefer the $10. Don't you?. Get something in the ground, plant it, invest it.

A MUST READ DIGEST FOR ALL! (Push To the finish Line)

11 DAYS COUNT DOWN
YOUR PRESENT AND FUTURE

EXPECTANCY

Expectancy reflects a level of faith, which is embedded in your belief system. I mentioned in prior writings, that everyone as a little bit of faith and it's not just owned by the religious community. What I want you to understand is that; expectancy does not work the same for everyone. If your neighbor or friend down the road, both started baking a turkey at the said time, they are both expecting the turkey will get done baking. Here is the difference. If your friend down the road goes to bed and leave the turkey in the oven, knowing it was still cooking, it's likely to get burned, dried out, and possible set the house on fire. On the other hand, your neighbor wanted to sleep, but because he/her cares so much about the turkey coming out right, and to place the garnish on top, they stayed up, monitor the turkey, and saw it to its completion.

Your neighbors' expectation will reflect a better outcome, because they invested time, and everything that was required to get a good turkey finish. The same process goes for any venture in life. If you plan a party, or you are holding a very important business meeting, and you invited 100 people, but you are expecting only 10 from the 100 people to show up, then such will be the case. The problem with such level of expectation is that, you do not believe in a few things. Your own power and might to make the event successful, the product ability to hold its value also, you have concluded to yourself, why all the 100 people will not show up. Because of your low expectation, you had 10 chairs set up, and when the event day came, all the 100 people showed up, except for 1 or 2, and you had no provision for them. You had no seats, no beverage or refreshments, no handouts or material for the event, and everything that indicates, failure and unprofessionalism was the order of the day.

This is a nonstarter, a formula for disaster, which will give you a bad reputation. Most time you only have once chance to impress others who are significant to you. This is even more important, when you are showing casing a product, or trying to solicit mew business partners, and sponsors for your business, or product line. Let them say, "You have gone above professionalism, and as shown them, what it really means to prepare for success. When the low expectancy happens, it may take you 1-5 years to recover from that downfall. Here is what expectancy for success looks like.

After your dreams have being discovered, and you are sure about the approach, you can begin tailoring the path with a sense of enthusiasm, and expects, or look forward to a great outcome, which will give new contacts, and monetarily gain. For a workshop, when there are 5o people on the invitation list, ask them to invite another person. For purpose of expecting others, including the initial 50 people, set up 100 chairs. Your seating arrangements could start from the front. When this happens, you can see all the empty chairs in the back, and the camera/video will only show those in the front and not the unoccupied chairs, should you choose to use a video recorder. In fact, you could also ask the hotel or conference space workers, to remove the extra chairs. You also want to make room for overflow, so that you will look professional at all times.

Get the name of your product or company on pens, booklets, pamphlets and possible little plastic bags.

A MUST READ DIGEST FOR ALL! (Push To the finish Line)

11 DAYS COUNT DOWN
YOUR PRESENT AND FUTURE

When people see that you are branded, and that you have a professional presents it gives you an edge among your competitors and it tells them you mean business. If you had advertise or offered to serve lunch or breakfast, make sure it's professionally done. A cheaper method is always to set up a buffet line. However for your guess or business mergers, CEO's, CFO's business owners, and other corporate executives, you must provide the highest standards of service, to create a lasting impression. You must get a wait team, or (service team) for functions of this nature. Let your potential business partners, sponsors and buyers, focus on your proposal or request, and not when their table will be announce to go and serve themselves.

DRESS FOR SUCCESS

I have to include this in the expectancy chapter, as a subtext. As important it is, to find the right venue, and cater very well, to have a good image for your prospects, you must have the dressing together to compliment everything that you have done or will be doing. Before anyone can see the setup of the room, taste the food, or go through the brochure and have a closer look at your offer, they sees your attire first. Do not where a red shirt, inside a blue jacket, with a black pants and a brown shoes, if you are a male. If you are a female, do not wear a flat loafer, with jeans pants, white blows inside and perhaps a quilt jacket. Please loose that right now. You must have a professional look, that tells them, you are ready to become a new business partner, or you are a professional who is ready to manage a win, win situation in your field of business. They are some colors and materials which is considered preferable, for business purposes. Here are some colors and possible materials.

Your colors should start and stop at blue, blue, grey, perhaps light brown or black, depending on the nature of business. When in doubt, go with blue or black. For the men, always wear black shoes. No blue shoes. You also need a 2 or three button suit, should you decide to wear one. You also need to focus on a light blue shirt or white. The tie needs to match the pants and no silk please. Let your tie, be all cotton, with a stripe pattern to match, or preferable plain. For women, wear black heels and you could get away with a blue. No velvet or open toe. You also want to focus on wearing a blue or black skirt that extends below the knee. Your prospects especially investors, may like the short skirt and does not mine seeing your thighs or legs, but they will not take you serious, even if your product line and or information looks very promising. Again, short skirt, with red heels and open front blows, might be the better attire if you are marketing perfume, or some sporty product, possibly Victoria Secret.

A professional look is still required, trying to get others to buy into your product and or services. If the women choose to wear a suit, choose a 1 button or 2 the most. This could be a pants or skirt suit. It is also recommend that you wear a full white shirt, and not a T-Shirt material insider. A tie could also be worn for the women, if it is short and blends in very well, with the suit. The hair of the women needs to be either comb in one with no glisten factors, or too much gel. If it needs to comb down to the shoulders, it must be plain as possible. The thing is, you do not want to create the image of a party girl. The men having a simple low hair cut will do. It could be wavy or just brush. When you are expecting a great outcome, for your dreams to come alive, you must put everything you have in it, and allow your mission to shine. It could be your only debut, to present you to the world.

A MUST READ DIGEST FOR ALL! (Push To the finish Line)

11 DAYS COUNT DOWN
YOUR PRESENT AND FUTURE

DETERMINATION

Show me some one, who has a business plan, or an idea for something great, but they have no determination. I would tell you; "that person is going nowhere". Determination ignites the strength of your power within. It creates drive, and drive plus determination equal results, and results plus drive, equals cash flow and immediate success. It could also be open doors, better opportunities, and super power connections. It starts with determination. Let's use the field of sports, to convey this point or message. Jamaica has the fastest man and woman in the world 2013. It was not always so for the Jamaicans. Perhaps if someone had told the country, such greatest would have happened one day, they would have disregarded it. Fraser Pryce from Jamaica ran her heart out to cross the finish line. Her excitement was delayed, because the race was narrowly won. She got excited after she looked at the score board, and realized that she was the winner and that she had set a new world record. Determination brought her there. I am sure there were many nights, running over those hills and mosquitoes bit her, as she made many attempts to kill them, She persevered to a champion.

I believe there were days, she wanted to give up, but she was determined to see her dreams come through. Usain Bolt, must have thought about the possibilities of loosing the race the very first time he ran. Although Jamaica had many sprinters over the years, perhaps they gave up on having the fastest in the world. I believe they must have matched Usain Bolt speed against the world record, and realized that Mr. Bolt speed either equals the world record during training or perhaps better some times. They must have thought, if he has better competition, and the pressure, he will be determine to run a faster race, because of his own desires to become a legend in the field of sprint racing. The world stood still and they watched, as Mr. Usain Bolt won the world title for Jamaica. This Island is the size of Connecticut in the USA, determination showed their strength. With determination, you can accomplish anything, and it does not depend on your race, culture, color, descendants, and so many other factors.

To succeed, determination is a required ingredient. There is no cake in the world you can bake, without flour. The same goes for a business, or a career, and sometimes building or buying a home. You must be determine. What does determination really means?. It means that you refuse to take no for an answer. It means that you are willing to look pass the negative possibilities or outcomes, and release a positive energy towards your goals and dreams expecting that they will come to fulfillment. Determination, allows you to stare down, fear, and doubt, disbelief, and those who does not believe in you, your product or your dreams, and tell them, I will prove you wrong. Determination allows a young lady, from Jamaica, this year of 2013 to enter a competition, called the VOICE and emerge as the winner. I learnt of this when the competition was over. I did not even know that anyone around the world, was welcome to participate. Determination as led the astronaut to the moon. Determination gives strength where weakness shows up, and tells you, no way, no how you are going to quit.

Determination pushes you to fight, for what you believe in, or at lease to allow your visions, dreams, aspirations and goals, to come alive and live. No company, from the Donald trump Empires, to the great New York City, could not be a success, or got built without the spirit of determination. The first plane that flew above ground took many trials and errors, but determination saw them through.

A MUST READ DIGEST FOR ALL! (Push To the finish Line)

11 DAYS COUNT DOWN
YOUR PRESENT AND FUTURE

FOLLOW THROUGH

This is a characteristic which is needed in every business person. In fact, in everyday activities, following through is a key element. Here is how follow through works. Let's use your brother or sister at home, and you are the eldest. You gave your little sister an instruction. You told her to go and wash dishes. After a few minutes or perhaps 45 minutes, you saw here playing somewhere in the home. You then asked her; "did you wash the dishes?" she replied "yes". You may even add; 'So why did you not inform me? The next step would be, to go to the kitchen and ensure the dishes were washed, as your sister said.   .

Following up or through, requires questions, or the need to inquire and then achieve. If you notice, the brother did not assume the washing of plate was completed. He asked a question, and indeed, questions produces answers. When you are in charge of anything, it is vitally important for you to implement the process of following through. The manager natural gives instruction and expects them to be carried out. If he/she does not personally check on the result or the outcome of the instructions given, the purpose would have being defeated. Very often, if the manager is not able to follow through, then a supervisor or someone empowered to check on the instructions, or job assignment, will report back to the manager of the outcome.

When you set up your business, or launch a new career, it is a must that you monitor the operations very closely. They are some reason for this. The investment or loan was given to you, and therefore you are required to distribute it correctly or appropriately in the business, for the sole purpose of a return profit. When there is a co-signer, things become more crucial for you, because the money was actually loan to the co-signer. That person is going to make sure, the business is going well, and that payments are made on time. The co-singer knows that if you do not pay back the loan, it is going to be there responsibility to pay it back. During the process of your operation, your eyes and initiatives must be involve 100%. Some of your employees, if you have employees, may not like it, but it is your investment, and you must protect it. You are required to have everything documented.

Every transaction needs to be reported. If a bill was paid for the company, if cash was used for personal reasons, if and when an employee got paid, if goods and services was paid for, and just about anything else that is included in the overhead operation. It does not matter If you have given another person the authority to act on your behalf, for a certain area of the business, it is imperative that you monitor that as well. To follow through on every area, and everything concerning the business, is a matter of you succeeding or failing. I should let you know, such actions of not monitoring things, always lead to disaster. Other individuals, does not know the sacrifice and the investment you have put in. They will never know, even if you tell them. There is an old time saying; "He who feels it, knows it", The same applies today, that because you were the one who did everything, where it started from your dream, it matters most to you, and that's why others could be a part of it later.

If you have a new career, it is your job to follow through. It simple means that you are required to pay attention to every instruction and assignments given to you. If you painted a picture, and sit it out to

A MUST READ DIGEST FOR ALL! (Push To the finish Line)

11 DAYS COUNT DOWN
YOUR PRESENT AND FUTURE

dry, do not ask another person to put it on display for you, or among the finish product, and walk away. It is your job, to check physically, if the person did what you had asked them to do. Many errors and major mistakes happen in companies and personal lives, all because someone did not follow through.

TRUST or STUPIDITY.

If you have employees, which may come along after the business gets established, they will say among private talks, "Does he/her trust us, and if so, why do you keep checking on the assignments given". Only someone not competent or a professional would feel this way. There is almost no baby boomer or senior person, who hires a contractor to do a particular job at home, and stay away from the work being done. They may even put a chair In the said area, and watch this contractor, from start to finish, to ensure the job is done correctly. I chuckled a smile or laughter, when I reflect on that scenery. In the business place, there is no time to watch employees in that manner, besides it would look too spooky, and can sometimes defeat the purpose, and soon no one wants to work for you. None the less, a system must be in place to monitor operations.

The stupidity aspect of this gesture is that, you trusted your cousin, to run the meat section of the little bill mart shop, down the road. You have never gone back there for anything, because in your mind, you trust him and want to see him do a good management job. Especially if he does not collect cash from customers, but just puts on the price and direct customers, where to pay. For such arrangements, you believe all is well. While you're trusting, cousin is stealing the meat out back, and selling it on the black market, as his friends come by and take it away, while he/her is still at work. Such actions, results in your cost going up, your profit margin becomes smaller, and if that section was the largest of your supplies and demands requirements, very soon you may have to close the business, while your cousin walks away with a smile on his/her face. Some People have seemingly killed their conscience.

I want you to read this very carefully. Sometimes, aunts, uncles, sisters, brothers, niece, nephews, mother, father, and cousins, makes bad business partners. If the business was already in the family, when you were born, then it is ok. However, if you are the one, who got a break through, and now you are trying to make something of yourself, and to raise the status of the family, let family stay away from your business. Use strangers, to whom you will give a little room, to help you carry out your goals. You need people, and that is a must. They are several screening which can be perform, to at least separates the criminals from the ones who may want to try and be an asset to your business. I am sure you will still monitor them, even with a 1000 back ground checks, and perhaps a camera or two in the work area. You are simple protecting your assets or investments. Security is never too much.

If your business is launched on the web, then obviously you may not need employees. However you must be aware, that they are hackers, who will try to get a portion of your investment, by stealing it. If your deposit from the web goes directly to an account, that you access all the time, change the pass word every 3 -7 days. I am just saying, if you want to protect your investments. Also it is wise to make sure that your website as a trusted certificate logo or symbol which is authentic. The more legit and professional presence you have on the web, could mean success, or a waste of time.

A MUST READ DIGEST FOR ALL! (Push To the finish Line)

11 DAYS COUNT DOWN
YOUR PRESENT AND FUTURE

NO MORE RESOLUTION

When I was growing up as a kid, every New Year, I would hear people making resolutions. It was only natural that I follow what they were doing. I cannot recall if any of those vows, pledge, promise, or gasp came through. The point I am making is that, resolutions are like pledges that everyone breaks. Yeah sure, they are a few that may try their very best endeavors, not to break or work towards them. It may last for a month or two, but then fades out, and everything goes right back to the norm. Quit making resolution, and have a set plan to work on. I really meant that. It is high time for people to realize, that to mix a resolution, with hope, and balance it on the equation of faith, is truly a nonstarter.

While having faith is important, and remaining hopeful is important, I am saying it is time to follow books like this one you are reading, and learn how to take charge of your life in the now, and make something great happen. They are so many dreams, desires, aspirations that needs to be empowered and break forth from your system, into a world of reality that brings forth substance. Resolutions or like promises and so often stirs up procrastination. You put things off in the moment of resolution, say' "for 2014 I am going to buy a house, I am going to have 10 children, I am going to get $10,000, I am going to be at work every day and stop calling off". For those who goes to church;" I am going to be at church every day, and make sure I do not miss a fasting service, so God can bless me". That statement is even selfish. Just read and revise that statement, it even sounds familiar to many of you. How many people keep these promises? .

Especially not calling off from work in the New Year and going to church every Sunday, Saturday, or whatever day is church for you. Stop making NEW Year Resolutions, and start working on an action plan. New Year Resolutions are short lived, and as no substance. It is time you create a plan, one that will create a path for good success. Resolutions are for future tense, which never gets off the ground for most people. You need the now action, and move forward with your dreams. You have procrastinated long enough, you have put off things long enough, you have told the future; "deposit this intention for me" too long. Let the present become tired of you. Do you know any inventors in your life? . For most of you, the answer will be no. Why don't you become your own inventor?. Every business objects, plans and money making venture, does not always require a lot of startup money.

When you need a new shirt, a peer of socks, bag, book, shoes a bike or a car, you will find the money to buy or fixed the one that was broken. If you need it bad enough, you will find a way to get it. Be hungry for success, become hungry to have wealth and riches, become hungry earn more, become hungry to find new connections that will help launch your dreams. Become hungry to be the best of what you can be, and who so ever you can be. My friends become hungry. I urge you, to become uncomfortable with your current situation. If you remain contented or seemingly happy in the current state where you are, nothing will change, but just allow you to repeat the same thing, year after year without any improvements. Let his be the year, you rise up from your slumber, you pick up a pen, you gather your phone numbers, you begin to touch the dial pad, you get connected to the internet, for business purpose, and let the quest begin. You spend so much time on Face-Book, Christian mingles, Google Plus, Tumb-r, Instagram, and Twitter. Where is the time and plan to invest in your future?

A MUST READ DIGEST FOR ALL! (Push To the finish Line)

11 DAYS COUNT DOWN
YOUR PRESENT AND FUTURE

CONCLUSION

Decades and centuries have pass, and so many of you from the time of your ancestors, to your own families, have never built a company, had a business, and launch anything for yourselves. You have only being taking and waiting for the crumbs to fall off the table. You do not have to wait for the crumbs any more. You do not have to settle. You can go forth and begin to take action, to change your future and those around you. As you have journeyed through the book, I hope you have discovered that, you are brighter, greater, and more special than you have thought before. I hope you have realized that the sky is the limit, and that you can be anything you want to be.

There is nothing so special about Angelina Jolie, or Brad Pitt, Oprah Winfrey or Joyce Myers. They did the same thing that you are just discovering, or is trying to get embedded in your system. They took a chance, went after their dreams, and look where it brought them. Some people, may just actual believe for a second, that some people were born to be poor, and others to be rich. This is very far from the truth. Jennifer Hudson did not make it back on time, for the final show down of the American Idol, and so perhaps, that was the reason why Fantasia Barrino won. Though that may have being the case, it was a good thing for Fantasia. Shortly after Jennifer Hudson found favor, with movie producers, and land herself a spot in the movies. If you think it, if you believe it, if you act on it, there is no reason why you cannot accomplish it.

Remember the first American idol winner, Kelly Clarkson. She left her home town and set out to discover her dreams wanting a change. She went to LA or Hollywood , and had was to sleep on cold concrete floor, waitress tables, got kick out of her house, perhaps because she could not pay the rent. She became homeless at one point, she could have returned home. She was however convince, there was something for her in LA or Hollywood that was going to change her life. She heard about the American Idol audition, and she went. The rest is history as she won, and a few years later she picked up 5 or more Grammy awards in 1 night. The worst injustice you can do to yourself, is not to initiate something right now, to change your destiny, and those who are personal connected to you.

Tyler Perry, the multi-Millionaire, was living out of his car. The first play he debut, called "Madea", no one showed up. The auditorium was empty. He kept at it, and did not gave up, until, the plays pulled enough traction, or become popular, which eventually went to the big screens. You know the rest of the story. If you did not understand anything, which was written in this book, and you are not impress, by the examples of those used, to challenge you, stop where you are. Look on the cover of this book. You can see its money decorated by the USA currency. If you do not have $300,000 of it, or $600,000 of it, or $1000000 worth of it; you are broke, and need to get up and do something about it. Search within for your dreams, and search for any desires, habits, or hobbies, that could be converted into cash, and make something specular great out of your life. Lastly, if you live pay check to pay check, and you just get enough from your employer to help pay the bills, and your bank account is negative, you are broke. If your method to financial independence is in a job, you are deceiving yourself, because you will never get to the "FIN" more so the "ANCIAL". Be wise, be smart, reach for great eights. See you at the top.

A MUST READ DIGEST FOR ALL! (Push To the finish Line)

11 DAYS COUNT DOWN
YOUR PRESENT AND FUTURE

MEET THE AUTHOR

Paul O.A Powell is a university graduate. He holds degrees in Hotel Management, computer science among others. He Majored in Apps development, Web development, and Software Architecture.

He is an author, who had the opportunity to have authored several books, under a different name, and this is his first book, release just using his maternal name, without a title or a syndicated name. He is radio talk-show personnel, motivational speaker, and a musician. He has written many songs, produced, and package as needed. He is yet to present his music to a recording label which he has never done before. Most of his music is released on a private label. He travels globally, and wants you to succeed as he has, and is still in the process of increasing his success and achievements. He is an entrepreneur, who as ran a hosting company, nonprofit organizations, and many online outlets. They are great things to come in 2014 from this young author and business man.

A MUST READ DIGEST FOR ALL! (Push To the finish Line)

11 DAYS COUNT DOWN
YOUR PRESENT AND FUTURE

Book Resource References Base

Chapters: Concepts/Proposals/Interpretations

SNAP OUT OF IT: The day dreaming concept.
DUJS, (2011), Science of Daydreaming, http://dujs.dartmouth.edu/fall-2010/science-of-daydreaming#.UrnmdPRDtGQ

IMAGINE: The Imagination Process.
Kares, (2008), Imagination, Urban Dictionary, http://www.urbandictionary.com/define.php?term=imaginate

IMAGINE: Effective imagination, leading to success.
K.Gibson,(2013),Define Cognitive Thinking, http://www.learningrx.com/define-cognitive-thinking-faq.htm

FOCUS : An attention getter to concentrate.
O. Dictionary,(2013), Definition of focus in English, http://www.oxforddictionaries.com/us/definition/american_english/focus

Dream: A challenge to let the voice of progress speaks. Discovering the power with in
J.Swan, (2002), who invented the lightbulb?, http://www.unmuseum.org/lightbulb.htm

Plant: Preparation concept for development.
P.Klein, A.Zaid, (ND, Internet), Land Preparation, Plantoing Operation, and fertilization Requirements, http://www.fao.org/docrep/006/y4360e/y4360e0a.htm

A MUST READ DIGEST FOR ALL! (Push To the finish Line)

11 DAYS COUNT DOWN
YOUR PRESENT AND FUTURE

A MUST READ DIGEST FOR ALL! (Push To the finish Line)

www.ingramcontent.com/pod-product-compliance
Lightning Source LLC
Chambersburg PA
CBHW081813170526
45167CB00008B/3428